ERIC FITCH DAGLISH (1892-1966)

was a wood engraver, writer

and illustrator. He learnt the art

of wood engraving from Paul

Nash and became known for his

illustrations of the natural world.

His book *Woodcuts of British Birds*

was published in 1925.